Fresh Vests to Knit

Knit year-round fashions with classic style—in these all-new texture
Edie Eckman's seven vests for women are true wardrobe boosters. W
with skirts or slacks, and dress them up or down. Each design gives ,
option to create your vest in a wide range of sizes, from X-Small to 2X-Large.
Make them for yourself, for family members, and your best friend. These
professionally designed garments will last and look amazing for years to come!

Meet the multitalented
EDIE ECKMAN

Years ago, Edie Eckman co-owned a yarn shop. The work severely limited her time to knit or crochet, so she closed the shop after a few years and turned to designing.

"Now I have my fingers in many aspects of the fiber arts," Edie says, and it's certainly true. She teaches her highly popular workshops, freelances as a technical editor for yarn craft magazines, and writes best-selling books on knitting and crochet. Edie's many titles include *How to Knit Socks: Three Methods Made Easy*, *Beyond the Square Crochet Motifs*, and *The Crochet Answer Book*.

"My family is very supportive of my travel-heavy life," Edie says. "My husband and our two children pitch in now and then to help with a deadline, but mostly they assist me every day by helping around the house while I stitch, pack, and prepare classes."

When developing knitting patterns, Edie doesn't design "on the needles."

"Occasionally," she says, "a design pops fully formed into my head, but it doesn't happen very often. Most of my creative process happens when I'm swatching. When I'm in 'design mode,' I keep my eyes open to inspiration everywhere—catalogs, the backyard, the tread on a tire. Once I'm trying out stitch patterns, the fabric I create begins to generate ideas. The finished swatch serves as my guide for sketching, pattern drafting, and knitting a sample."

Even before her multifaceted career was established, Edie already had faith in her creative instincts.

"My most challenging knitting project was a multi-colored intarsia vest designed by Sasha Kagan," says Edie. "It was twenty-five years ago. I had knit only two sweaters in my life, and those were just one color. Off I bopped to the yarn shop to buy the fingering weight yarn and 3.25 mm needles required. If I had asked the shop owner, she would have steered me to something easier based on my experience, but it never occurred to me to ask.

"I struggled to knit that vest and it turned out beautifully. I still have it, and show it off in some of the classes I teach. To me, it's an example of not allowing skill level designations keep you from making what you want. 'Too hard' patterns are a chance to ramp up my knitting skills and push myself to learn faster."

So how does Edie unplug from the working world?

"We have a little cabin in the woods near a lake. There's no TV or Internet service. I love to go there and do nothing. I take the dog for walks and paddle around the lake. Even any deadline-related knitting/crocheting I do there is relaxing.

"However, being a freelance editor means I'm always looking for the next editing job. Also, I've always got designs in my head ready to be sold, and there's at least another book or two in the future."

To keep up with Edie and check her workshop schedule for upcoming events, visit her Web site at EdieEckman.com.

LEISURE ARTS, INC.
Little Rock, Arkansas

artful argyle

Size	Finished Chest Measurement
X-Small	31¹/₂" (80 cm)
Small	35" (89 cm)
Medium	39" (99 cm)
Large	43¹/₂" (110.5 cm)
X-Large	47¹/₂" (120.5 cm)
2X-Large	51" (129.5 cm)

Size Note: Instructions are written with sizes X-Small, Small, and Medium in the first set of braces { } and sizes Large, X-Large, and 2X-Large in the second set of braces. Instructions will be easier to read if you circle all the numbers pertaining to your size. If only one number is given, it applies to all sizes.

MATERIALS

Medium Weight Yarn
[3.5 ounces, 220 yards
(100 grams, 200 meters) per ball]:
  Blue - {3-3-4}{4-5-5} balls
  Lt Green - 1 ball
  Green - 1 ball
Straight knitting needles, size 8
  (5 mm) **or** size needed for gauge
16" (40.5 cm) Circular knitting
  needle, size 7 (4.5 mm)
Markers - 6
Stitch holder
Yarn needle

GAUGE: With larger size needles, in Stockinette Stitch (knit one row, purl one row), 19 sts and 26 rows = 4" (10 cm)

Techniques Used:
• K2 tog *(Fig. 6, page 39)*
• P2 tog *(Fig. 9, page 39)*
• SSK *(Figs. 7a-c, page 39)*

BACK
RIBBING
With larger size needles and Blue, cast on {77-85-95}{105-115-123} sts.

Row 1: K1, (P1, K1) across.

Row 2 (Right side): P1, (K1, P1) across.

Repeat Rows 1 and 2 until Ribbing measures 1" (2.5 cm), ending by working Row 1.

BODY
Beginning with a **knit** row, work in Stockinette Stitch until piece measures approximately {2-2-2¼}{2¹/₂-2¹/₂-2¹/₂}"/{5-5-5.5}{6.5-6.5-6.5} cm from cast on edge, ending by working a **purl** row.

Next Row: K {10-14-17}{22-25-29} sts, place marker *(see Markers, page 38)*, K 13 following Chart 1 *(Fig. 2, page 38)*, place marker, ★ K {9-9-11}{11-13-13}, place marker, K 13 following Chart 1, place marker; repeat from ★ once **more**, knit across.

Continue working in Stockinette Stitch following Chart 1 between markers as established until all Chart rows are complete and removing markers on last row.

CHART 1

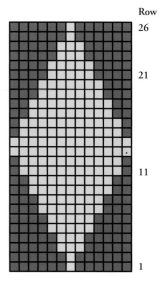

Work even until piece measures approximately {13³/₄-14¹/₂-15}{15-15-15¹/₄}"/{35-37-38}{38-38-38.5} cm from cast on edge, ending by working a **purl** row.

ARMHOLE SHAPING
Maintain established pattern throughout.

Rows 1 and 2: Bind off {4-5-6}{7-8-10} sts, work across: {69-75-83}{91-99-103} sts.

Instructions continued on page 4.

Row 3 (Decrease row): K1, SSK, knit across to last 3 sts, K2 tog, K1: {67-73-81}{89-97-101} sts.

Row 4: Purl across.

Repeat Rows 3 and 4, {3-5-5}{7-10-10} times: {61-63-71}{75-77-81} sts.

Work even until Armholes measure approximately {7¼-7½-8}{8½-9-9¼}"/{18.5-19-20.5}{21.5-23-23.5} cm, ending by working a **purl** row.

NECK AND SHOULDER SHAPING

Both sides of Neck are worked at the same time, using separate yarn for **each** side.

Row 1: Bind off {6-6-7}{7-7-8} sts, knit across until there are {13-13-15}{17-17-17} sts on the right needle; with second yarn, bind off next {23-25-27}{27-29-31} sts, knit across.

Row 2: Bind off {6-6-7}{7-7-8} sts, purl across; with second yarn, purl across: {13-13-15}{17-17-17} sts **each** side.

Rows 3 and 4: Bind off {5-5-6}{7-7-7} sts, work across; with second yarn, bind off 3 sts, work across: {5-5-6}{7-7-7} sts **each** side.

Row 5: Bind off remaining sts on first side; with second yarn, work across.

Bind off remaining sts.

FRONT

Work same as Back to Armhole Shaping.

ARMHOLE AND V-NECK SHAPING

Both sides of Neck are worked at the same time, using separate yarn for **each** side.

Row 1: Bind off {4-5-6}{7-8-10} sts, knit across: {73-80-89}{98-107-113} sts.

Row 2: Bind off {4-5-6}{7-8-10} sts, purl across until there are {34-37-41}{45-49-51} sts on the right needle, slip next st onto st holder; with second yarn, purl across: {34-37-41}{45-49-51} sts **each** side.

Row 3 (Decrease row): K1, SSK, knit across to within 3 sts of Neck edge, K2 tog, K1; with second yarn, K1, SSK, knit across to last 3 sts, K2 tog, K1: {32-35-39}{43-47-49} sts **each** side.

Continue to decrease one stitch at each Armhole edge in same manner, every other row, {3-5-5}{7-10-10} times **more** AND AT THE SAME TIME decrease one stitch at **each** Neck edge, every other row, {7-8-8}{7-7-8} times **more**; then decrease every fourth row, {6-6-7}{8-9-9} times: {16-16-19}{21-21-22} sts **each** side.

Work even until Armholes measure same as Back to Shoulder Shaping, ending by working a **purl** row.

SHOULDER SHAPING

Rows 1 and 2: Bind off {6-6-7}{7-7-8} sts, work across; with second yarn, work across: {10-10-12}{14-14-14} sts **each** side.

Rows 3 and 4: Bind off {5-5-6}{7-7-7} sts, work across; with second yarn, work across: {5-5-6}{7-7-7} sts **each** side.

Row 5: Bind off remaining sts on first side leaving a long end for sewing; with second yarn, work across.

Bind off remaining sts, leaving a long end for sewing.

FINISHING

With long ends, sew shoulder seams.

DUPLICATE STITCH

With Green, duplicate stitch lines as shown on Chart 2 as follows: Each knit stitch forms a V and you want to completely cover that V, so that the design appears to have been knit into the sweater. Each square on a chart represents one knit stitch that is to be covered by a Duplicate Stitch.

Thread a yarn needle with an 18" (45.5 cm) length of yarn. Beginning at lower right of the design and with **right** side facing, bring the needle up from the **wrong** side at the base of the V, leaving an end to be woven in later (never tie knots). The needle should always go **between** the strands of yarn. Follow the right side of the V up and insert the needle from **right** to **left** under the legs of the V immediately above it, keeping the yarn on top of the stitch **(Fig. A)**, and draw through. Follow the left side of the V back down to the base and insert the needle back through the bottom of the same stitch where the first stitch began **(Fig. B, Duplicate Stitch completed)**. Continuing to follow chart, bring needle up through the next stitch. Repeat for each stitch, keeping tension even with tension of knit fabric to avoid puckering. When a length of yarn is finished, run it under several stitches on **back** of work to secure.

Fig. A

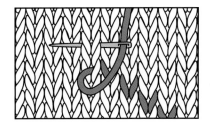

Fig. B

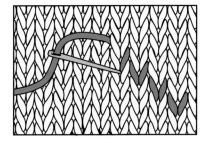

CHART 2

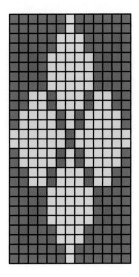

Weave side seams (*Fig. 13, page 40*).

NECKBAND

With **right** side facing, using circular needle, Blue, and beginning at right shoulder seam, pick up {33-35-37} {37-39-41} sts evenly spaced across Back Neck edge (*Figs. 11a & b, page 40*), pick up {31-33-35} {37-39-41} sts evenly spaced across left Front Neck edge to st holder, place marker, knit st from st holder, pick up {31-33-35}{37-39-41} sts evenly spaced across right Front Neck edge, place marker to mark beginning of round: {96-102-108} {112-118-124} sts.

Rnd 1 (Decrease rnd): (K1, P1) across to within 2 sts of marker, SSK, K1, K2 tog, P1, (K1, P1) around: {94-100-106} {110-116-122} sts.

Rnd 2: (K1, P1) across to within one st of marker, K3, P1, (K1, P1) around.

Rnd 3 (Decrease rnd): K1, (P1, K1) across to within 2 sts of marker, P2 tog, K1, P2 tog, (K1, P1) around: {92-98-104}{108-114-120} sts.

Rnd 4: (K1, P1) around.

Rnd 5: Repeat Rnd 1: {90-96-102} {106-112-118} sts.

Bind off all sts in pattern.

ARMHOLE BAND

With **right** side facing, using circular needle and Blue, pick up {74-76-80} {86-90-92} sts evenly spaced around one Armhole edge, beginning at side seam, place marker to mark beginning of round.

Work in K1, P1 ribbing for 5 rnds.

Bind off all sts in pattern.

Repeat around remaining Armhole.

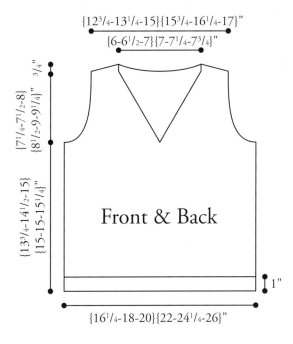

{12³/₄-13¹/₄-15}{15³/₄-16¹/₄-17}"

{6-6¹/₂-7}{7-7¹/₄-7³/₄}"

³/₄"

{7¹/₄-7¹/₂-8}
{8¹/₂-9-9¹/₄}"

{13³/₄-14¹/₂-15}
{15-15-15¹/₄}"

Front & Back

1"

{16¹/₄-18-20}{22-24¹/₄-26}"

Note: Vest includes two edge stitches.

5

fresh idea

Size	Finished Chest Measurement
X-Small	31$^1/_2$" (80 cm)
Small	34$^3/_4$" (88.5 cm)
Medium	39$^3/_4$" (100.5 cm)
Large	41" (104 cm)
X-Large	47$^1/_2$" (120.5 cm)
2X-Large	50$^3/_4$" (129 cm)

Size Note: Instructions are written with sizes X-Small, Small, and Medium in the first set of braces { } and sizes Large, X-Large, and 2X-Large in the second set of braces. Instructions will be easier to read if you circle all the numbers pertaining to your size. If only one number is given, it applies to all sizes.

MATERIALS
Medium Weight Yarn [3 ounces, 145 yards (85 grams, 132 meters) per skein]:
    Blue - {3-4-4}{5-5-6} skeins
    Tan - {3-4-4}{5-5-6} skeins
Straight knitting needles, size 8 (5 mm) **or** size needed for gauge
16" (40.5 cm) Circular knitting needle, size 7 (4.5 mm)
Stitch holder
Marker
Yarn needle

GAUGE: With larger size needles, in pattern, 20 sts and 30 rows = 4" (10 cm)

Gauge Swatch: 4$^1/_4$"w x 4"h (10.75 cm x 10 cm)
With larger size needles and Blue, cast on 21 sts.
Row 1: Purl across; drop Blue.
Rows 2-30: Work same as Back, beginning with Row 14.
Bind off all sts.

Techniques Used:
- K2 tog (*Fig. 6, page 39*)
- SSK (*Figs. 7a-c, page 39*)
- P2 tog (*Fig. 9, page 39*)
- SSP (*Fig. 10, page 40*)

BACK
With larger size needles and Blue, cast on {81-89-101} {105-121-129} sts.

Row 1: Knit across, drop Blue.

Carry unused color along edge of piece.

Row 2 (Right side)**:** With Tan, K4, WYB slip 1 as if to **purl**, ★ K3, WYB slip 1 as if to **purl**; repeat from ★ across to last 4 sts, K4.

Row 3: P1, K3, ★ WYF slip 1 as if to **purl**, K3; repeat from ★ across to last st, P1; drop Tan.

Row 4: With Blue, K2, WYB slip 1 as if to **purl**, ★ K3, WYB slip 1 as if to **purl**; repeat from ★ across to last 2 sts, K2.

Row 5: P1, K1, WYF slip 1 as if to **purl**, ★ K3, WYF slip 1 as if to **purl**; repeat from ★ across to last 2 sts, K1, P1; drop Blue.

Rows 6-12: Repeat Rows 2-5 once, then repeat Rows 2-4 once **more**.

Row 13: P2, WYF slip 1 as if to **purl**, ★ P3, WYF slip 1 as if to **purl**; repeat from ★ across to last 2 sts, P2; drop Blue.

Row 14: With Tan, K4, WYB slip 1 as if to **purl**, ★ K3, WYB slip 1 as if to **purl**; repeat from ★ across to last 4 sts, K4.

Row 15: P4, WYF slip 1 as if to **purl**, ★ P3, WYF slip 1 as if to **purl**; repeat from ★ across to last 4 sts, P4; drop Tan.

Row 16: With Blue, K2, WYB slip 1 as if to **purl**, ★ K3, WYB slip 1 as if to **purl**; repeat from ★ across to last 2 sts, K2.

Repeat Rows 13-16 for pattern until piece measures approximately {13$^3/_4$-14$^1/_2$-15}{15-15-15$^1/_4$}"/ {35-37-38}{38-38-38.5} cm from cast on edge, ending by working a **wrong** side row.

Instructions continued on page 8.

fresh idea

ARMHOLE SHAPING

Maintain established pattern throughout.

Rows 1 and 2: Bind off {4-6-7} {7-9-10} sts, work across: {73-77-87} {91-103-109} sts.

Row 3 (Decrease row)**:** K1, SSK, work across to last 3 sts, K2 tog, K1: {71-75-85}{89-101-107} sts.

Continue to decrease one stitch at **each** edge, every other row, {3-4-5} {6-10-11} times **more:** {65-67-75}{77-81-85} sts.

Work even until Armholes measure approximately {7$\frac{1}{4}$-7$\frac{1}{2}$-8} {8$\frac{1}{2}$-9-9$\frac{1}{4}$}"/{18.5-19-20.5} {21.5-23-23.5} cm, ending by working a **wrong** side row.

NECK AND SHOULDER SHAPING

Both sides of Neck are worked at the same time, using separate yarn for each side.

Row 1: Bind off {5-5-6}{7-8-7} sts, work across until there are {15-15-17}{17-17-19} sts on right needle; with second yarn, bind off next {25-27-29}{29-31-33} sts, work across.

Row 2: Bind off {5-5-6}{7-8-7} sts, work across; with second yarn, work across: {15-15-17}{17-17-19} sts **each** side.

Rows 3 and 4: Bind off {6-6-7} {7-7-8} sts, work across; with second yarn, bind off 3 sts, work across: {6-6-7}{7-7-8} sts **each** side.

Row 5: Bind off remaining sts on first side; with second yarn, work across.

Bind off remaining sts.

FRONT

Work same as Back to Armhole Shaping.

NECK AND ARMHOLE SHAPING

Both sides of Neck are worked at the same time, using separate yarn for each side.

Row 1: Bind off {4-6-7}{7-9-10} sts, work across until there are {36-38-43}{45-51-54} sts on the right needle, slip next st onto st holder; with second yarn, work across.

Row 2: Bind off {4-6-7}{7-9-10} sts, work across; with second yarn, work across: {36-38-43}{45-51-54} sts **each** side.

Row 3 (Decrease row)**:** K1, SSK, knit across to within 3 sts of Neck edge, K2 tog, K1; with second yarn, K1, SSK, knit across to last 3 sts, K2 tog, K1: {34-36-41}{43-49-52} sts **each** side.

Continue to decrease one stitch at each Armhole edge in same manner, every other row, {3-4-5} {6-10-11} times **more** AND AT THE SAME TIME decrease one stitch at **each** Neck edge, every other row, {3-4-4}{2-2-3} times **more**; then decrease every fourth row, {11-11-12} {14-15-15} times: {17-17-20} {21-22-23} sts **each** side.

Work even until Armholes measure same as Back to Shoulder Shaping, ending by working a **wrong** side row.

SHOULDER SHAPING

Rows 1 and 2: Bind off {5-5-6} {7-8-7} sts, work across; with second yarn, work across: {12-12-14} {14-14-16} sts **each** side.

Rows 3 and 4: Bind off {6-6-7} {7-7-8} sts, work across; with second yarn, work across: {6-6-7}{7-7-8} sts **each** side.

Row 5: Bind off remaining sts on first side leaving a long end for sewing; with second yarn, work across.

Bind off remaining sts, leaving a long end for sewing.

FINISHING

With long ends, sew shoulder seams.

Weave side seams *(Fig. 13, page 40)*.

NECK TRIM

With **right** side facing, using circular needle, Blue, and beginning at right shoulder seam, pick up {35-37-39} {39-41-43} sts evenly spaced across Back Neck edge *(Figs. 11a & b, page 40)*, pick up {37-38-40} {42-45-46} sts evenly spaced across left Front Neck edge to center st, place marker, slip center st from st holder onto left point of circular needle and knit it, pick up {37-38-40}{42-45-46} sts evenly spaced across right Front Neck edge, place marker to mark beginning of round *(see Markers, page 38)*: {110-114-120}{124-132-136} sts.

Rnd 1: Purl across to within 2 sts of marker, SSP, remove marker, P1, P2 tog, purl around: {108-112-118} {122-130-134} sts.

Bind off all sts in **knit**.

ARMHOLE TRIM

With **right** side facing, using circular needle and Blue, pick up {70-72-76} {80-84-88} sts evenly spaced around one Armhole edge.

Rnd 1: Purl around.

Bind off all sts in **knit**.

Repeat around remaining Armhole.

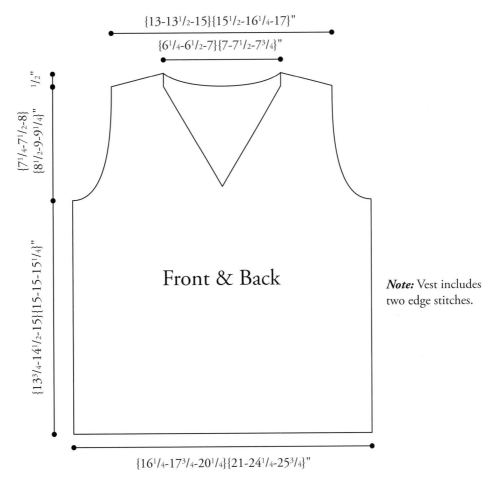

{13-13½-15}{15½-16¼-17}"

{6¼-6½-7}{7-7½-7¾}"

½"

{7¼-7½-8}{8½-9-9¼}"

{13¾-14½-15}{15-15-15¼}"

Front & Back

Note: Vest includes two edge stitches.

{16¼-17¾-20¼}{21-24¼-25¾}"

casual charm

Size	Finished Chest Measurement	
X-Small	31^1/$_2$"	(80 cm)
Small	35"	(89 cm)
Medium	39^1/$_2$"	(100.5 cm)
Large	43"	(109 cm)
X-Large	48"	(122 cm)
2X-Large	52"	(132 cm)

Size Note: Instructions are written with sizes X-Small, Small, and Medium in the first set of braces { } and sizes Large, X-Large, and 2X-Large in the second set of braces. Instructions will be easier to read if you circle all the numbers pertaining to your size. If only one number is given, it applies to all sizes.

MATERIALS

Medium Weight Yarn
[1^3/$_4$ ounces, 110 yards
(50 grams, 101 meters) per skein]:
{6-7-8}{9-10-11} skeins
Straight knitting needles, size 8
(5 mm) **or** size needed for gauge
Double pointed needles,
size 7 (4.5 mm) for Trim
Yarn needle

GAUGE: With larger size needles, in pattern, 20 sts = 4^1/$_4$" (10.75 cm); 28 rows = 4"(10 cm)

Gauge Swatch: 4^1/$_4$"w x 4"h
(10.75 cm x 10 cm)
Cast on 20 sts.

Rows 1-28: Repeat Rows 1 and 2 of Back, 14 times.
Bind off all sts.

Techniques Used:
• K1 tbl *(Fig. 1, page 38)*
• M1 *(Figs. 4a & b, page 38)*
• K2 tog *(Fig. 6, page 39)*
• SSK *(Figs. 7a-c, page 39)*

BACK

Cast on {86-95-104}
{113-125-131} sts.

Row 1: Knit across.

Row 2 (Right side): P2, (K1 tbl, P2) across.

Rows 3-6: Repeat Rows 1 and 2 twice.

Row 7 (Decrease row): K1, SSK, knit across to last 3 sts, K2 tog, K1: {84-93-102}{111-123-129} sts.

Row 8: P1, K1 tbl, (P2, K1 tbl) across to last st, P1.

Row 9: Knit across.

Rows 10-12: Repeat Rows 8 and 9 once, then repeat Row 8 once **more**.

Row 13: Repeat Row 7: {82-91-100} {109-121-127} sts.

Row 14: P3, K1 tbl, (P2, K1 tbl) across to last 3 sts, P3.

Row 15: Knit across.

Rows 16-18: Repeat Rows 14 and 15 once, then repeat Row 14 once **more**.

Row 19: Repeat Row 7: {80-89-98} {107-119-125} sts.

Row 20: P2, (K1 tbl, P2) across.

Row 21: Knit across.

Rows 22-24: Repeat Rows 20 and 21 once, then repeat Row 20 once **more**.

Rows 25-49: Repeat Rows 7-24 once, then repeat Rows 7-13 once **more**: {70-79-88}{97-109-115} sts.

Repeat Rows 14 and 15 until Back measures approximately {7^1/$_4$-7^1/$_4$-7^1/$_4$}{7^1/$_2$-7^1/$_2$-7^3/$_4$}"/ {18.5-18.5-18.5}{19-19-19.5} cm from cast on edge, ending by working Row 14.

BUST SHAPING

Row 1 (Increase row): K1, M1, knit across to last st, M1, K1: {72-81-90} {99-111-117} sts.

Row 2: P1, K1 tbl, (P2, K1 tbl) across to last st, P1.

Row 3: Knit across.

Rows 4-10: Repeat Rows 2 and 3, 3 times; then repeat Row 2 once **more**.

Row 11: Repeat Row 1: {74-83-92} {101-113-119} sts.

Instructions continued on page 12.

casual charm

Row 12: P2, (K1 tbl, P2) across.

Row 13: Knit across.

Rows 14-20: Repeat Rows 12 and 13, 3 times; then repeat Row 12 once **more**.

Row 21: Repeat Row 1: {76-85-94}{103-115-121} sts.

Row 22: P3, K1 tbl, (P2, K1 tbl) across to last 3 sts, P3.

Row 23: Knit across.

Sizes Medium, Large, and 2X-Large Only
Rows 24-30: Repeat Rows 22 and 23, 3 times; then repeat Row 22 once **more**.

Rows 31-33: Repeat Rows 1-3: {96}{105-123} sts.

All Sizes
Repeat last 2 rows until Back measures approximately {13$\frac{3}{4}$-14$\frac{1}{2}$-15}{15-15-15$\frac{1}{4}$}"/{35-37-38}{38-38-38.5} cm from cast on edge, ending by working a **knit** row.

ARMHOLE SHAPING
Maintain established pattern throughout.

Rows 1 and 2: Bind off {4-5-6}{7-8-9} sts, work across: {68-75-84}{91-99-105} sts.

Sizes X-Large and 2X-Large Only
Rows 3 and 4: Bind off 2 sts, work across: {95-101} sts.

Size 2X-Large Only
Rows 5 and 6: Bind off 2 sts, work across: 97 sts.

All Sizes
Next Row: Work across.

Decrease Row: K1, SSK, knit across to last 3 sts, K2 tog, K1: {66-73-82}{89-93-95} sts.

Repeat last 2 rows, {2-4-5}{7-8-8} times: {62-65-72}{75-77-79} sts.

Work even until Armholes measure approximately {7$\frac{1}{4}$-7$\frac{1}{2}$-8}{8$\frac{1}{2}$-9-9$\frac{1}{4}$}"/{18.5-19-20.5}{21.5-23-23.5} cm, ending by working a **right** side row.

SHOULDER AND NECK SHAPING
Both sides of Neck are worked at the same time, using separate yarn for each side.

Row 1: Bind off {5-6-6}{7-7-7} sts, knit across until there are {15-15-17}{17-17-17} sts on the right needle; with second yarn, bind off next {22-23-26}{27-29-31} sts, knit across.

Row 2: Bind off {5-6-6}{7-7-7} sts, work across; with second yarn, work across: {15-15-17}{17-17-17} sts **each** side.

Rows 3 and 4: Bind off {6-6-7}{7-7-7} sts, work across; with second yarn, bind off 3 sts, work across: {6-6-7}{7-7-7} sts **each** side.

Row 5: Bind off remaining sts on first side; with second yarn, knit across.

Bind off remaining sts.

RIGHT FRONT
Cast on {43-47-51}{55-63-67} sts.

Row 1: Knit across.

Row 2 (Right side): (P2, K1 tbl) across to last {1-2-3}{1-3-1} st(s), P {1-2-3}{1-3-1}.

Rows 3-6: Repeat Rows 1 and 2 twice.

Row 7 (Decrease row): K1, SSK, knit across: {42-46-50}{54-62-66} sts.

Row 8: (P2, K1 tbl) across to last {3-1-2}{3-2-3} st(s), P {3-1-2}{3-2-3}.

Row 9: Knit across.

Rows 10-12: Repeat Rows 8 and 9 once, then repeat Row 8 once **more**.

Row 13: Repeat Row 7: {41-45-49}{53-61-65} sts.

Row 14: (P2, K1 tbl) across to last {2-3-1}{2-1-2} st(s), P {2-3-1}{2-1-2}.

Row 15: Knit across.

Rows 16-18: Repeat Rows 14 and 15 once, then repeat Row 14 once **more**.

Row 19: Repeat Row 7: {40-44-48}{52-60-64} sts.

Row 20: (P2, K1 tbl) across to last {1-2-3}{1-3-1} st(s), P {1-2-3}{1-3-1}.

Row 21: Knit across.

Rows 22-24: Repeat Rows 20 and 21 once, then repeat Row 20 once **more**.

Rows 25-49: Repeat Rows 7-24 once, then repeat Rows 7-13 once **more**: {35-39-43}{47-55-59} sts.

Repeat Rows 14 and 15 until Right Front measures approximately {7¼-7¼-7¼}{7½-7½-7¾}"/ {18.5-18.5-18.5}{19-19-19.5} cm from cast on edge, ending by working a **right** side row.

BUST SHAPING

Row 1 (Increase row): K1, M1, knit across: {36-40-44}{48-56-60} sts.

Row 2: (P2, K1 tbl) across to last {3-1-2}{3-2-3} st(s), P {3-1-2}{3-2-3}.

Row 3: Knit across.

Rows 4-10: Repeat Rows 2 and 3, 3 times; then repeat Row 2 once **more**.

Row 11: Repeat Row 1: {37-41-45} {49-57-61} sts.

Row 12: (P2, K1 tbl) across to last {1-2-3}{1-3-1} st(s), P {1-2-3}{1-3-1}.

Row 13: Knit across.

Rows 14-20: Repeat Rows 12 and 13, 3 times; then repeat Row 12 once **more**.

Row 21: Repeat Row 1: {38-42-46} {50-58-62} sts.

Row 22: (P2, K1 tbl) across to last {2-3-1}{2-1-2} st(s), P {2-3-1}{2-1-2}.

Row 23: Knit across.

Sizes Medium, Large, and 2X-Large Only
Rows 24-30: Repeat Rows 22 and 23, 3 times; then repeat Row 22 once **more**.

Rows 31-33: Repeat Rows 1-3: {47} {51-63} sts.

All Sizes
Repeat last 2 rows until Right Front measures same as Back to Armhole

Shaping, ending by working a **right** side row.

ARMHOLE AND NECK SHAPING
Maintain established pattern throughout.

Row 1: Bind off {4-5-6} {7-8-9} sts, knit across: {34-37-41} {44-50-54} sts.

Row 2: Work across.

Sizes X-Large and 2X-Large Only
Row 3: Bind off 2 sts, knit across: {48-52} sts.

Row 4: Work across.

Size 2X-Large Only
Rows 5 and 6: Repeat Rows 3 and 4: 50 sts.

All Sizes
Decrease Row: K1, SSK, knit across: {33-36-40}{43-47-49} sts.

Continue to decrease one stitch at Armhole edge in same manner, every other row, {2-4-5}{7-8-8} times **more** AND AT THE SAME TIME when Armhole measures approximately {2¼-2½-2½}{3-3-3¼}"/ {5.5-6.5-6.5}{7.5-7.5-8.5} cm, decrease one stitch at Neck edge, every other row, {12-12-12} {12-16-20} times; then decrease every fourth row, {2-2-3}{3-2-0} times **more** (**see Zeros, page 38**): {17-18-20}{21-21-21} sts.

Work even until Armhole measures same as Back to Shoulder Shaping, ending by working a **right** side row.

SHOULDER SHAPING
Row 1: Bind off {5-6-6} {7-7-7} sts, knit across: {12-12-14} {14-14-14} sts.

Row 2: Work across.

Row 3: Bind off {6-6-7}{7-7-7} sts, knit across: {6-6-7}{7-7-7} sts.

Row 4: Work across.

Bind off remaining sts, leaving a long end for sewing.

LEFT FRONT
With straight needles, cast on {43-47-51}{55-63-67} sts.

Row 1: Knit across.

Row 2 (Right side): P {1-2-3}{1-3-1}, (K1 tbl, P2) across.

Rows 3-6: Repeat Rows 1 and 2 twice.

Row 7 (Decrease row): Knit across to last 3 sts, K2 tog, K1: {42-46-50} {54-62-66} sts.

Row 8: P {3-1-2}{3-2-3}, (K1 tbl, P2) across.

Row 9: Knit across.

Rows 10-12: Repeat Rows 8 and 9 once, then repeat Row 8 once **more**.

Row 13: Repeat Row 7: {41-45-49} {53-61-65} sts.

Row 14: P {2-3-1}{2-1-2}, (K1 tbl, P2) across.

Row 15: Knit across.

Rows 16-18: Repeat Rows 14 and 15 once, then repeat Row 14 once **more**.

Instructions continued on page 14.

Row 19: Repeat Row 7: {40-44-48} {52-60-64} sts.

Row 20: P {1-2-3}{1-3-1}, (K1 tbl, P2) across.

Row 21: Knit across.

Rows 22-24: Repeat Rows 20 and 21 once, then repeat Row 20 once **more**.

Rows 25-49: Repeat Rows 7-24 once, then repeat Rows 7-13 once **more**: {35-39-43}{47-55-59} sts.

Repeat Rows 14 and 15 until Left Front measures approximately {7^1/$_4$-7^1/$_4$-7^1/$_4$}{7^1/$_2$-7^1/$_2$-7^3/$_4$}"/ {18.5-18.5-18.5}{19-19-19.5} cm from cast on edge, ending by working a **right** side row.

BUST SHAPING

Row 1 (Increase row): Knit across to last st, M1, K1: {36-40-44} {48-56-60} sts.

Row 2: P {3-1-2}{3-2-3}, (K1 tbl, P2) across.

Row 3: Knit across.

Rows 4-10: Repeat Rows 2 and 3, 3 times; then repeat Row 2 once **more**.

Row 11: Repeat Row 1: {37-41-45} {49-57-61} sts.

Row 12: P {1-2-3}{1-3-1}, (K1 tbl, P2) across.

Row 13: Knit across.

Rows 14-20: Repeat Rows 12 and 13, 3 times; then repeat Row 12 once **more**.

Row 21: Repeat Row 1: {38-42-46} {50-58-62} sts.

Row 22: P {2-3-1}{2-1-2}, (K1 tbl, P2) across.

Row 23: Knit across.

Sizes Medium, Large, and 2X-Large Only
Rows 24-30: Repeat Rows 22 and 23, 3 times; then repeat Row 22 once **more**.

Rows 31-33: Repeat Rows 1-3: {47} {51-63} sts.

All Sizes
Repeat last 2 rows until Left Front measures same as Right Front to Armhole Shaping, ending by working a **knit** row.

ARMHOLE AND NECK SHAPING
Maintain established pattern throughout.

Row 1: Bind off {4-5-6} {7-8-9} sts, work across: {34-37-41} {44-50-54} sts.

Row 2: Knit across.

Sizes X-Large and 2X-Large Only
Row 3: Bind off 2 sts, work across: {48-52} sts.

Row 4: Knit across.

Size 2X-Large Only
Rows 5 and 6: Repeat Rows 3 and 4: 50 sts.

All Sizes
Next Row: Work across.

Decrease Row: Knit across to last 3 sts, K2 tog, K1: {33-36-40} {43-47-49} sts.

Continue to decrease one stitch at Armhole edge in same manner, every other row, {2-4-5}{7-8-8} times **more** AND AT THE SAME TIME when Armhole measures approximately {2^1/$_4$-2^1/$_2$-2^1/$_2$}{3-3-3^1/$_4$}"/ {5.5-6.5-6.5}{7.5-7.5-8.5} cm, decrease one stitch at Neck edge, every other row, {12-12-12} {12-16-20} times; then decrease every fourth row, {2-2-3}{3-2-0} times **more**: {17-18-20}{21-21-21} sts.

Work even until Armhole measures same as Right Front to Shoulder Shaping, ending by working a **knit** row.

SHOULDER SHAPING
Row 1: Bind off {5-6-6} {7-7-7} sts, work across: {12-12-14} {14-14-14} sts.

Row 2: Knit across.

Row 3: Bind off {6-6-7}{7-7-7} sts, work across: {6-6-7}{7-7-7} sts.

Row 4: Knit across.

Bind off remaining sts, leaving a long end for sewing.

FINISHING

With long ends, sew shoulder seams.

Weave side seams *(Fig. 13, page 40)*.

TRIM
ARMHOLE

With double pointed needles, cast on 3 sts.

With **wrong** side facing, pick up one st at underarm seam *(Figs. 11a & b, page 40)*, do **not** turn, slide sts to opposite end of needle: 4 sts.

★ K2, SSK, pick up one st on edge, slide sts to opposite end of needle; repeat from ★ around, skipping sts or rows as necessary so that the Trim lies flat.

Bind off all sts in **knit**, leaving a long end for sewing.

With long end, sew ends of Trim together.

Repeat around second Armhole.

FRONT AND NECK

With double pointed needles, cast on 3 sts.

With **wrong** side facing, pick up one st at bottom of Left Front, do **not** turn, slide sts to opposite end of needle: 4 sts.

★ K2, SSK, pick up one st on edge, slide sts to opposite end of needle; repeat from ★ to bottom of Right Front, skipping sts or rows as necessary so that the Trim lies flat.

Bind off all sts in **knit**.

TIE (Make 2)

With double pointed needles, cast on 3 sts.

★ K3, slide sts to opposite end of needle; repeat from ★ until Tie measures 10" (25.5 cm).

Bind off all sts in **knit**, leaving a long end for sewing.

Using photo as a guide, sew one Tie to each Front, knotting opposite end. Note that the pattern is reversible.

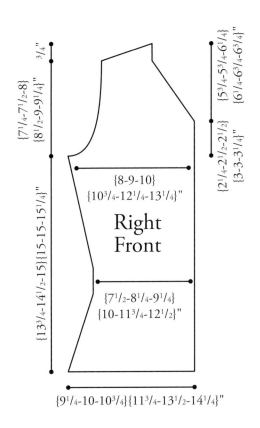

Note: Vest includes two edge stitches.

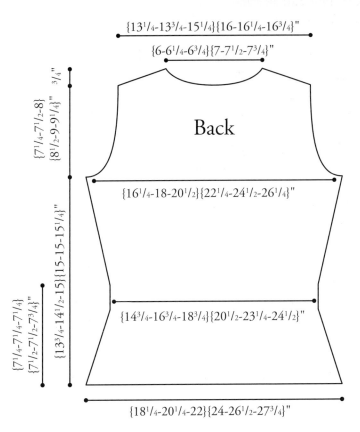

clever classic

Size	Finished Chest Measurement
X-Small	30" (76 cm)
Small	34" (86.5 cm)
Medium	38" (96.5 cm)
Large	42" (106.5 cm)
X-Large	46" (117 cm)
2X-Large	50" (127 cm)

Size Note: Instructions are written with sizes X-Small, Small, and Medium in the first set of braces { } and sizes Large, X-Large, and 2X-Large in the second set of braces. Instructions will be easier to read if you circle all the numbers pertaining to your size. If only one number is given, it applies to all sizes.

MATERIALS

Medium Weight Yarn **(4)** [3 ounces, 185 yards (85 grams, 170 meters) per skein]: {4-4-5}{5-6-6} skeins
Straight knitting needles, sizes 7 (4.5 mm) **and** 8 (5 mm) **or** sizes needed for gauge
16" (40.5 cm) Circular knitting needle, size 7 (4.5 mm)
Marker
Yarn needle

GAUGE: With larger size needles, in pattern, 20 sts and 22 rows = 4" (10 cm)

Gauge Swatch: 5^1/$_2$"w x 4"h (14 cm x 10 cm)
With larger size needles, cast on 27 sts.
Work same as Back for 22 rows.
Bind off all sts.

Techniques Used:
• K2 tog *(Fig. 6, page 39)*
• SSK *(Figs. 7a-c, page 39)*

BACK
RIBBING

With smaller size straight needles, cast on {77-87-97}{107-117-127} sts.

Row 1: K1, (P1, K1) across.

Row 2: P1, (K1, P1) across.

Repeat Rows 1 and 2 until Ribbing measures approximately 6" (15 cm) from cast on edge.

BODY

Change to larger size needles.

Row 1 (Right side): ★ (K3, P1) twice, K1, P1; repeat from ★ across to last 7 sts, K3, P1, K3.

Row 2: ★ (P3, K1) twice, P1, K1; repeat from ★ across to last 7 sts, P3, K1, P3.

Row 3: K2, P1, K1, P1, ★ (K3, P1) twice, K1, P1; repeat from ★ across to last 2 sts, K2.

Row 4: P2, K1, P1, K1, ★ (P3, K1) twice, P1, K1; repeat from ★ across to last 2 sts, P2.

Row 5: K1, ★ (P1, K1) twice, (P1, K2) twice; repeat from ★ across to last 6 sts, (P1, K1) 3 times.

Row 6: (P1, K1) 3 times, ★ (P2, K1) twice, (P1, K1) twice; repeat from ★ across to last st, P1.

Row 7: K2, P1, K1, P1, ★ (K3, P1) twice, K1, P1; repeat from ★ across to last 2 sts, K2.

Row 8: P2, K1, P1, K1, ★ (P3, K1) twice, P1, K1; repeat from ★ across to last 2 sts, P2.

Rows 9 and 10: Repeat Rows 1 and 2.

Row 11: K3, P1, ★ K2, P1, (K1, P1) twice, K2, P1; repeat from ★ across to last 3 sts, K3.

Row 12: P3, K1, ★ P2, K1, (P1, K1) twice, P2, K1; repeat from ★ across to last 3 sts, P3.

Repeat Rows 1-12 for pattern until piece measures approximately {12^3/$_4$-13^1/$_2$-14}{14-14-14^1/$_4$}"/ {32.5-34.5-35.5}{35.5-35.5-36} cm from cast on edge, ending by working a **wrong** side row.

Instructions continued on page 18.

ARMHOLE SHAPING

Maintain established pattern throughout.

Rows 1 and 2: Bind off {4-5-6} {8-10-11} sts, work across: {69-77-85}{91-97-105} sts.

Row 3 (Decrease row): K1, SSK, work across to last 3 sts, K2 tog, K1: {67-75-83}{89-95-103} sts.

Row 4: Work across.

Rows 5 thru {8-12-14}{18-22-24}: Repeat Rows 3 and 4, {2-4-5} {7-9-10} times: {63-67-73} {75-77-83} sts.

Work even until Armholes measure approximately {7¼-7½-8} {8½-9-9¼}"/{18.5-19-20.5} {21.5-23-23.5} cm, ending by working a **wrong** side row.

NECK AND SHOULDER SHAPING

Both sides of Neck are worked at the same time, using separate yarn for each side.

Row 1: Bind off {6-5-7}{6-6-8} sts, work across until there are {13-15-15}{17-17-17} sts on right needle; with second yarn, bind off next {25-27-29}{29-31-33} sts, work across.

Row 2: Bind off {6-5-7}{6-6-8} sts, work across; with second yarn, work across: {13-15-15}{17-17-17} sts **each** side.

Rows 3 and 4: Bind off {5-6-6} {7-7-7} sts, work across; with second yarn, bind off 3 sts, work across: {5-6-6}{7-7-7} sts **each** side.

Row 5: Bind off remaining sts on first side; with second yarn, work across.

Bind off remaining sts.

FRONT

Work same as Back through Row {6-8-8}{10-10-12} of Armhole Shaping: {65-71-79}{83-89-95} sts.

NECK SHAPING

Both sides of Neck are worked at the same time, using separate yarn for each side.

Row 1: K1, SSK, work across until there are {26-28-31}{33-35-37} sts on right needle; with second yarn, bind off next {11-13-15} {15-17-19} sts, work across to last 3 sts, K2 tog, K1: {26-28-31} {33-35-37} sts **each** side.

Row 2: Work across; with second yarn, bind off 3 sts, work across.

Size X-Small Only
Row 3: Work across; with second yarn, bind off 3 sts, work across: 23 sts **each** side.

Rows 4 and 5: Work across; with second yarn, bind off 2 sts, work across: 21 sts **each** side.

Row 6: Work across; with second yarn, work across.

Row 7 (Decrease row): Work across to within 3 sts of Neck edge, K2 tog, K1; with second yarn, K1, SSK, work across: 20 sts **each** side.

Rows 8-15: Repeat Rows 6 and 7, 4 times: 16 sts **each** side.

Size Small Only
Row 3: K1, SSK, work across; with second yarn, bind off 3 sts, work across to last 3 sts, K2 tog, K1: 24 sts **each** side.

Rows 4-15: Work same as Size X-Small: 17 sts **each** side.

Size Medium Only
Row 3: K1, SSK, work across; with second yarn, bind off 3 sts, work across to last 3 sts, K2 tog, K1: 27 sts **each** side.

Row 4: Work across; with second yarn, bind off 2 sts, work across.

Row 5: K1, SSK, work across; with second yarn, bind off 2 sts, work across to last 3 sts, K2 tog, K1: 24 sts **each** side.

Rows 6-15: Work same as Size X-Small: 19 sts **each** side.

Sizes Large, X-Large, and 2X-Large Only
Row 3: K1, SSK, work across; with second yarn, bind off 3 sts, work across to last 3 sts, K2 tog, K1: {29-31-33} sts **each** side.

Row 4: Work across; with second yarn, bind off 2 sts, work across.

Row 5: K1, SSK, work across; with second yarn, bind off 2 sts, work across to last 3 sts, K2 tog, K1: {26-28-30} sts **each** side.

Row 6: Work across; with second yarn, work across.

Row 7 (Decrease row): K1, SSK, work across to within 3 sts of Neck edge, K2 tog, K1; with second yarn, K1, SSK, work across to last 3 sts, K2 tog, K1: {24-26-28} sts **each** side.

Row 8: Work across; with second yarn, work across.

Size Large Only
Row 9 (Decrease row): Work across to within 3 sts of Neck edge, K2 tog, K1; with second yarn, K1, SSK, work across: 23 sts **each** side.

Rows 8-15: Repeat Rows 8 and 9, 3 times: 20 sts **each** side.

Sizes X-Large and 2X-Large Only
Rows 9-12: Repeat Rows 7 and 8 twice: {22-24} sts **each** side.

Row 13 (Decrease row): Work across to within 3 sts of Neck edge, K2 tog, K1; with second yarn, K1, SSK, work across: {21-23} sts **each** side.

Row 14: Work across; with second yarn, work across.

Rows 15 and 16: Repeat Rows 13 and 14: {20-22} sts **each** side.

All Sizes
Work even until Armholes measure same as Back to Shoulder Shaping, ending by working a **wrong** side row.

SHOULDER SHAPING

Rows 1 and 2: Bind off {6-5-7}{6-6-8} sts, work across; with second yarn, work across: {10-12-12}{14-14-14} sts **each** side.

Rows 3 and 4: Bind off {5-6-6}{7-7-7} sts, work across; with second yarn, work across: {5-6-6}{7-7-7} sts **each** side.

Row 5: Bind off remaining sts on first side, leaving a long end for sewing; with second yarn, work across.

Bind off remaining sts, leaving a long end for sewing.

FINISHING
With long ends, sew shoulder seams.

Weave side seams **(Fig. 13, page 40)**.

NECK RIBBING
With **right** side facing, using circular needle, and beginning at right shoulder, pick up {37-39-41}{41-43-45} sts evenly spaced across Back Neck edge **(Figs. 11a & b, page 40)**, pick up {34-33-35}{35-36-36} sts evenly spaced across left Front Neck edge, pick up {11-13-15}{15-17-19} sts across bound off sts on Front, pick up {34-33-35}{35-36-36} sts evenly spaced across right Front Neck edge, place marker to mark beginning of round: {116-118-126}{126-132-136} sts.

Work in K1, P1 ribbing until Ribbing measures approximately 1" (2.5 cm).

Bind off all sts in ribbing.

ARMHOLE RIBBING
With **right** side facing, using circular needle, and beginning at side seam, pick up {54-56-60}{64-68-70} sts evenly spaced around one Armhole edge, place marker to mark beginning of round.

Work in K1, P1 ribbing until Ribbing measures approximately 1" (2.5 cm).

Bind off all sts in ribbing.

Repeat around remaining Armhole.

{12½-13½-14½}{15-15½-16½}"
{6¼-6½-7}{7-7½-7¾}"

{7¼-7½-8}{8½-9-9¼}" 1"
{6¼-6-6½}{6½-7-7}"
{1-1½-1½}{2-2-2¼}"

Front & Back

{12¾-13½-14}{14-14-14¼}"

6"

{15½-17½-19½}{21½-23½-25½}"

Note: Vest includes two edge stitches.

lighthearted

Size	Finished Chest Measurement	
X-Small	30³/₄"	(78 cm)
Small	35¹/₂"	(90 cm)
Medium	38³/₄"	(98.5 cm)
Large	42¹/₂"	(108 cm)
X-Large	46³/₄"	(121 cm)
2X-Large	50¹/₂"	(128.5 cm)

Size Note: Instructions are written with sizes X-Small, Small, and Medium in the first set of braces { } and sizes Large, X-Large, and 2X-Large in the second set of braces. Instructions will be easier to read if you circle all the numbers pertaining to your size. If only one number is given, it applies to all sizes.

MATERIALS

Medium Weight Yarn 〔④〕
[4 ounces, 186 yards
(113 grams, 170 meters)
per skein]:
  {4-4-5}{5-6-7} skeins
Straight knitting needles, size 8
  (5 mm) **or** size needed for gauge
16" (40.5 cm) **and** 32" (81.5 cm)
  Circular knitting needles,
  size 7 (4.5 mm)
Marker
Yarn needle

GAUGE: With larger size needles, in Stockinette Stitch (knit one row, purl one row), 18 sts and 24 rows = 4" (10 cm)

Techniques Used:
- YO *(Fig. 3, page 38)*
- K2 tog *(Fig. 6, page 39)*
- SSK *(Figs. 7a-c, page 39)*
- Slip 1 as if to **knit**, K2 tog, PSSO *(Fig. 8, page 39)*
- P2 tog *(Fig. 9, page 39)*
- SSP *(Fig. 10, page 40)*

BACK

With larger size needles, cast on {87-99-111}{111-123-135} sts.

Row 1: Knit across.

Row 2 (Right side)**:** K4, YO, slip 1 as if to **knit**, K2 tog, PSSO, YO, (K3, YO, slip 1 as if to **knit**, K2 tog, PSSO, YO) {6-7-8}{8-9-10} times, K1, YO, slip 1 as if to **knit**, K2 tog, PSSO, YO, (K3, YO, slip 1 as if to **knit**, K2 tog, PSSO, YO) across to last 4 sts, K4.

Row 3: Purl across.

Row 4: K3, ★ YO, slip 1 as if to **knit**, K2 tog, PSSO, YO, K3; repeat from ★ across.

Row 5: Purl across.

Row 6: K2, YO, slip 1 as if to **knit**, K2 tog, PSSO, YO, (K3, YO, slip 1 as if to **knit**, K2 tog, PSSO, YO) {6-7-8}{8-9-10} times, K5, YO, slip 1 as if to **knit**, K2 tog, PSSO, YO, (K3, YO, slip 1 as if to **knit**, K2 tog, PSSO, YO) across to last 2 sts, K2.

Row 7: Purl across.

Row 8: K1, YO, slip 1 as if to **knit**, K2 tog, PSSO, YO, (K3, YO, slip 1 as if to **knit**, K2 tog, PSSO, YO) {6-7-8}{8-9-10} times, K7, YO, slip 1 as if to **knit**, K2 tog, PSSO, YO, (K3, YO, slip 1 as if to **knit**, K2 tog, PSSO, YO) across to last st, K1.

Rows 9-11: Purl across.

Row 12: K3, (K2 tog, YO, K4) across.

Row 13: Purl across.

Row 14: K2, K2 tog, YO, K1, YO, SSK, (K1, K2 tog, YO, K1, YO, SSK) across to last 2 sts, K2.

Row 15: Purl across.

Row 16 (Decrease row)**:** K1, SSK, knit across to last 3 sts, K2 tog, K1: {85-97-109}{109-121-133} sts.

Row 17: Purl across.

Instructions continued on page 22.

lighthearted

Row 18: K5, K2 tog, YO, (K4, K2 tog, YO) across to last 6 sts, K6.

Row 19: Purl across.

Row 20: K4, K2 tog, YO, K1, YO, SSK, (K1, K2 tog, YO, K1, YO, SSK) across to last 4 sts, K4.

Row 21: Purl across.

Sizes X-Small, Small, Medium, and 2X-Large Only
Row 22: Repeat Row 16: {83-95-107}{131} sts.

Row 23: Purl across.

Row 24: K1, K2 tog, YO, (K4, K2 tog, YO) across to last 2 sts, K2.

Row 25: Purl across.

Row 26: K3, YO, SSK, K1, K2 tog, YO, (K1, YO, SSK, K1, K2 tog, YO) across to last 3 sts, K3.

Size X-Small Only
Row 27: Purl across.

Row 28: Knit across.

Row 29: Purl across.

Row 30: K1, SSK, K1, K2 tog, YO, (K4, K2 tog, YO) across to last 5 sts, K2, K2 tog, K1: 81 sts.

Row 31: Purl across.

Row 32: K2, K2 tog, YO, K1, YO, SSK, (K1, K2 tog, YO, K1, YO, SSK) across to last 2 sts, K2.

Beginning with a **purl** row, work in Stockinette Stitch, decreasing one stitch at **each** edge in same manner, every eighth row, 5 times **more**: 71 sts.

Sizes Small, Medium, and 2X-Large Only
Rows 27-29: Repeat Rows 21-23: {93-105}{129} sts.

Row 30: K3, (K2 tog, YO, K4) across.

Row 31: Purl across.

Row 32: K2, K2 tog, YO, K1, YO, SSK, (K1, K2 tog, YO, K1, YO, SSK) across to last 2 sts, K2.

Beginning with a **purl** row, work in Stockinette Stitch, decreasing one stitch at **each** edge in same manner, every sixth row, {1-8}{3} time(s) **more**; then decrease every eighth row, {5-0}{4} times **(see Zeros, page 38)**: {81-89}{115} sts.

Sizes Large and X-Large Only
Row 22: Knit across.

Row 23: Purl across.

Row 24: K1, SSK, K5, K2 tog, YO, (K4, K2 tog, YO) across to last 3 sts, K2 tog, K1: {107-119} sts.

Row 25: Purl across.

Row 26: K3, YO, SSK, K1, K2 tog, YO, (K1, YO, SSK, K1, K2 tog, YO) across to last 3 sts, K3.

Row 27: Purl across.

Row 28: Knit across.

Row 29: Purl across.

Row 30: (K4, K2 tog, YO) across to last 5 sts, K5.

Row 31: Purl across.

Row 32: K1, SSK, K2 tog, YO, K1, YO, SSK, (K1, K2 tog, YO, K1, YO, SSK) across to last 3 sts, K2 tog, K1: {105-117} sts.

Beginning with a **purl** row, work in Stockinette Stitch, decreasing one stitch at **each** edge in same manner, every eighth row, {4-5} times **more**: {97-107} sts.

All Sizes
Work even until Back measures approximately {13³/₄-14¹/₂-15} {15-15-15¹/₄}"/{35-37-38} {38-38-38.5} cm from cast on edge, ending by working a **purl** row.

ARMHOLE SHAPING

Maintain established pattern throughout.

Rows 1 and 2: Bind off {4-5-6} {7-9-9} sts, work across: {63-71-77} {83-89-97} sts.

Row 3: Knit across.

Row 4 (Decrease row): P1, P2 tog, purl across to last 3 sts, SSP, P1: {61-69-75}{81-87-95} sts.

Repeat Rows 3 and 4, {1-4-4}{6-8-9} time(s): {59-61-67}{69-71-77} sts.

Work even until Armholes measure approximately {7$\frac{1}{4}$-7$\frac{1}{2}$-8} {8$\frac{1}{2}$-9-9$\frac{1}{4}$}"/{18.5-19-20.5} {21.5-23-23.5} cm, ending by working a **purl** row.

SHOULDER AND NECK SHAPING

Both sides of Neck are worked at the same time, using separate yarn for each side.

Row 1: Bind off 6 sts, knit across until there are {13-13-15} {15-15-17} sts on the right needle; with second yarn, bind off next {21-23-25}{27-29-31} sts, knit across.

Row 2: Bind off 6 sts, purl across; with second yarn, purl across: {13-13-15}{15-15-17} sts **each** side.

Rows 3 and 4: Bind off {5-5-6} {6-6-7} sts, work across; with second yarn, bind off 3 sts, work across: {5-5-6}{6-6-7} sts **each** side.

Row 5: Bind off remaining sts on first side; with second yarn, knit across.

Bind off remaining sts.

RIGHT FRONT

With larger size needles, cast on {44-50-56}{56-62-68} sts.

Row 1: Knit across.

Row 2 (Right side): K4, YO, slip 1 as if to **knit**, K2 tog, PSSO, YO, (K3, YO, slip 1 as if to **knit**, K2 tog, PSSO, YO) across to last st, K1.

Row 3: Purl across.

Row 4: (K3, YO, slip 1 as if to **knit**, K2 tog, PSSO, YO) across to last 2 sts, K2.

Row 5: Purl across.

Row 6: K2, (YO, slip 1 as if to **knit**, K2 tog, PSSO, YO, K3) across.

Row 7: Purl across.

Row 8: K1, YO, slip 1 as if to **knit**, K2 tog, PSSO, YO, (K3, YO, slip 1 as if to **knit**, K2 tog, PSSO, YO) across to last 4 sts, K4.

Rows 9-11: Purl across.

Row 12: K3, K2 tog, YO, (K4, K2 tog, YO) across to last 3 sts, K3.

Row 13: Purl across.

Row 14: K2, (K2 tog, YO, K1, YO, SSK, K1) across.

Row 15: Purl across.

Row 16 (Decrease row): Knit across to last 3 sts, K2 tog, K1: {43-49-55} {55-61-67} sts.

Row 17: Purl across.

Row 18: K6, K2 tog, YO, (K4, K2 tog, YO) across to last 5 sts, K5.

Row 19: Purl across.

Row 20: K5, K2 tog, YO, K1, YO, SSK, (K1, K2 tog, YO, K1, YO, SSK) across to last 3 sts, K3.

Row 21: Purl across.

Sizes X-Small, Small, Medium, and 2X-Large Only
Row 22: Repeat Row 16: {42-48-54} {66} sts.

Row 23: Purl across.

Instructions continued on page 24.

Row 24: K3, K2 tog, YO, (K4, K2 tog, YO) across to last 7 sts, K7.

Row 25: Purl across.

Row 26: K2, K2 tog, YO, K1, YO, SSK, (K1, K2 tog, YO, K1, YO, SSK) across to last 5 sts, K5.

Size X-Small Only
Row 27: Purl across.

Row 28: Knit across.

Row 29: Purl across.

Row 30: K6, K2 tog, YO, (K4, K2 tog, YO) across to last 4 sts, K1, K2 tog, K1: 41 sts.

Row 31: Purl across.

Row 32: K5, (K2 tog, YO, K1, YO, SSK, K1) across.

Beginning with a **purl** row, work in Stockinette Stitch, decreasing one stitch at **same** edge in same manner, every eighth row, 5 times **more**: 36 sts.

Sizes Small, Medium, and 2X-Large Only
Rows 27-29: Repeat Rows 21-23: {47-53}{65} sts.

Row 30: K6, K2 tog, YO, (K4, K2 tog, YO) across to last 3 sts, K3.

Row 31: Purl across.

Row 32: K5, (K2 tog, YO, K1, YO, SSK, K1) across.

Beginning with a **purl** row, work in Stockinette Stitch, decreasing one stitch at **same** edge in same manner, every sixth row, {1-8}{3} time(s) **more**; then decrease every eighth row, {5-0}{4} times: {41-45}{58} sts.

Sizes Large and X-Large Only
Row 22: Knit across.

Row 23: Purl across.

Row 24: K3, K2 tog, YO, (K4, K2 tog, YO) across to last 8 sts, K5, K2 tog, K1: {54-60} sts.

Row 25: Purl across.

Row 26: K2, K2 tog, YO, K1, YO, SSK, (K1, K2 tog, YO, K1, YO, SSK) across to last 5 sts, K5.

Row 27: Purl across.

Row 28: Knit across.

Row 29: Purl across.

Row 30: K6, (K2 tog, YO, K4) across.

Row 31: Purl across.

Row 32: K5, K2 tog, YO, K1, YO, SSK, (K1, K2 tog, YO, K1, YO, SSK) across to last 2 sts, K2 tog: {53-59} sts.

Beginning with a **purl** row, work in Stockinette Stitch, decreasing one stitch at **same** edge in same manner, every eighth row, {4-5} times **more**: {49-54} sts.

All Sizes
Work even until Right Front measures same as Back to Armhole Shaping, ending by working a **knit** row.

ARMHOLE AND NECK SHAPING
Maintain established pattern throughout.

Row 1: Bind off {4-5-6} {7-9-9} sts, purl across: {32-36-39} {42-45-49} sts.

Row 2: Knit across.

Row 3 (Decrease row): P1, P2 tog, purl across: {31-35-38} {41-44-48} sts.

Continue to decrease one stitch at Armhole edge in same manner, every other row, {1-4-4}{6-8-9} time(s) **more** AND AT THE SAME TIME when Armhole measures approximately 2^1/$_2$" (6.5 cm), decrease one stitch at Neck edge, every other row, {14-15-16} {17-18-19} times: {16-16-18} {18-18-20} sts.

Work even until Armhole measures same as Back to Shoulder Shaping, ending by working a **knit** row.

SHOULDER SHAPING
Row 1: Bind off 6 sts, purl across: {10-10-12}{12-12-14} sts.

Row 2: Knit across.

Row 3: Bind off {5-5-6}{6-6-7} sts, purl across: {5-5-6}{6-6-7} sts.

Row 4: Knit across.

Bind off remaining sts, leaving a long end for sewing.

LEFT FRONT

With larger size needles, cast on {44-50-56}{56-62-68} sts.

Row 1: Knit across.

Row 2 (Right side)**:** K1, YO, slip 1 as if to **knit**, K2 tog, PSSO, YO, (K3, YO, slip 1 as if to **knit**, K2 tog, PSSO, YO) across to last 4 sts, K4.

Row 3: Purl across.

Row 4: K2, (YO, slip 1 as if to **knit**, K2 tog, PSSO, YO, K3) across.

Row 5: Purl across.

Row 6: (K3, YO, slip 1 as if to **knit**, K2 tog, PSSO, YO) across to last 2 sts, K2.

Row 7: Purl across.

Row 8: K4, YO, slip 1 as if to **knit**, K2 tog, PSSO, YO, (K3, YO, slip 1 as if to **knit**, K2 tog, PSSO, YO) across to last st, K1.

Rows 9-11: Purl across.

Row 12: K2, (K2 tog, YO, K4) across.

Row 13: Purl across.

Row 14: (K1, K2 tog, YO, K1, YO, SSK) across to last 2 sts, K2.

Row 15: Purl across.

Row 16 (Decrease row)**:** K1, SSK, knit across: {43-49-55}{55-61-67} sts.

Row 17: Purl across.

Row 18: (K4, K2 tog, YO) across to last 7 sts, K7.

Row 19: Purl across.

Row 20: K3, K2 tog, YO, K1, YO, SSK, (K1, K2 tog, YO, K1, YO, SSK) across to last 5 sts, K5.

Row 21: Purl across.

Sizes X-Small, Small, Medium, and 2X-Large Only

Row 22: Repeat Row 16: {42-48-54}{66} sts.

Row 23: Purl across.

Row 24: K6, (K2 tog, YO, K4) across.

Row 25: Purl across.

Row 26: K5, K2 tog, YO, K1, YO, SSK, (K1, K2 tog, YO, K1, YO, SSK) across to last 2 sts, K2.

Instructions continued on page 26.

Size X-Small Only

Row 27: Purl across.

Row 28: Knit across.

Row 29: Purl across.

Row 30: K1, SSK, K2 tog, YO, (K4, K2 tog, YO) across to last 7 sts, K7: 41 sts.

Row 31: Purl across.

Row 32: (K1, K2 tog, YO, K1, YO, SSK) across to last 5 sts, K5.

Beginning with a **purl** row, work in Stockinette Stitch, decreasing one stitch at **same** edge in same manner, every eighth row, 5 times **more**: 36 sts.

Sizes Small, Medium, and 2X-Large Only

Rows 27-29: Repeat Rows 21-23: {47-53}{65} sts.

Row 30: K2, K2 tog, YO, (K4, K2 tog, YO) across to last 7 sts, K7.

Row 31: Purl across.

Row 32: (K1, K2 tog, YO, K1, YO, SSK) across to last 5 sts, K5.

Beginning with a **purl** row, work in Stockinette Stitch, decreasing one stitch at **same** edge in same manner, every sixth row, {1-8}{3} time(s) **more**; then decrease every eighth row, {5-0}{4} times: {41-45}{58} sts.

Sizes Large and X-Large Only

Row 22: Knit across.

Row 23: Purl across.

Row 24: K1, SSK, K4, (K2 tog, YO, K4) across: {54-60} sts.

Row 25: Purl across.

Row 26: K5, K2 tog, YO, K1, YO, SSK, (K1, K2 tog, YO, K1, YO, SSK) across to last 2 sts, K2.

Row 27: Purl across.

Row 28: Knit across.

Row 29: Purl across.

Row 30: K3, K2 tog, YO, (K4, K2 tog, YO) across to last 7 sts, K7.

Row 31: Purl across.

Row 32: SSK, K2 tog, YO, K1, YO, SSK, (K1, K2 tog, YO, K1, YO, SSK) across to last 5 sts, K5: {53-59} sts.

Beginning with a **purl** row, work in Stockinette Stitch, decreasing one stitch at **same** edge in same manner, every eighth row, {4-5} times **more**: {49-54} sts.

All Sizes

Work even until Left Front measures same as Right Front to Armhole Shaping, ending by working a **purl** row.

ARMHOLE AND NECK SHAPING

Maintain established pattern throughout.

Row 1: Bind off {4-5-6} {7-9-9} sts, knit across: {32-36-39} {42-45-49} sts.

Row 2: Purl across.

Row 3 (Decrease row): K1, SSK, knit across: {31-35-38}{41-44-48} sts.

Continue to decrease one stitch at Armhole edge in same manner, every other row, {1-4-4}{6-8-9} time(s) **more** AND AT THE SAME TIME when Armhole measures approximately 2$\frac{1}{2}$" (6.5 cm), decrease one stitch at Neck edge, every other row, {14-15-16} {17-18-19} times: {16-16-18} {18-18-20} sts.

Work even until Armhole measures same as Right Front to Shoulder Shaping, ending by working a **purl** row.

SHOULDER SHAPING

Row 1: Bind off 6 sts, knit across: {10-10-12}{12-12-14} sts.

Row 2: Purl across.

Row 3: Bind off {5-5-6}{6-6-7} sts, knit across: {5-5-6}{6-6-7} sts.

Row 4: Purl across.

Bind off remaining sts, leaving a long end for sewing.

FINISHING

With long ends, sew shoulder seams.

Weave side seams *(Fig. 13, page 40)*.

FRONT EDGING

With **right** side facing and using 32" (81.5 cm) circular needle, pick up {84-86-88}{90-92-94} sts evenly spaced across Right Front edge to shoulder seam *(Figs. 11a & b, page 40)*, pick up {23-25-27}{29-31-33} sts evenly spaced across Back Neck edge, pick up {84-86-88}{90-92-94} sts evenly spaced across Left Front edge: {191-197-203}{209-215-221} sts.

Row 1: Knit across.

Row 2 (Eyelet row): K2, (YO, K2 tog, K1) across.

Row 3: Knit across.

Bind off all sts in **knit**.

ARMHOLE EDGING

With **right** side facing, using 16" (40.5 cm) circular needle, and beginning at side seam, pick up {60-63-66}{69-72-75} sts evenly spaced around one Armhole edge, place marker to mark beginning of round *(see Markers, page 38)*.

Rnd 1: Purl around.

Rnd 2: (K2 tog, YO, K1) around.

Rnd 3: Purl around.

Bind off all sts in **knit**.

Repeat around remaining Armhole.

Note: Vest incudes two edge stitches.

Back

{13-13¹/₂-15}{15¹/₄-15³/₄-17}"

{6-6¹/₂-7}{7¹/₄-7³/₄-8¹/₄}"

{7¹/₄-7¹/₂-8}{8¹/₂-9-9¹/₄}" ³/₄"

{13³/₄-14¹/₂-15}{15-15-15¹/₄}"

{15³/₄-18-19³/₄}{21¹/₂-23³/₄-25¹/₂}"

{19¹/₄-22-24³/₄}{24³/₄-27¹/₄-30}"

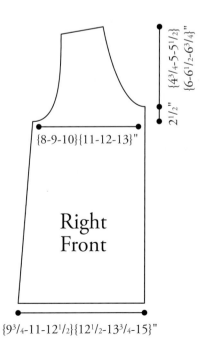

Right Front

{4³/₄-5-5¹/₂}{6-6¹/₂-6³/₄}"

2¹/₂"

{8-9-10}{11-12-13}"

{9³/₄-11-12¹/₂}{12¹/₂-13³/₄-15}"

27

fun & breezy

⬤■☐☐ EASY +

Size	Finished Chest Measurement	
X-Small	32¹/₂"	(82.5 cm)
Small	36"	(91.5 cm)
Medium	39¹/₂"	(100.5 cm)
Large	45"	(114.5 cm)
X-Large	48¹/₂"	(123 cm)
2X-Large	52"	(132 cm)

Size Note: Instructions are written with sizes X-Small, Small, and Medium in the first set of braces { } and sizes Large, X-Large, and 2X-Large in the second set of braces. Instructions will be easier to read if you circle all the numbers pertaining to your size. If only one number is given, it applies to all sizes.

MATERIALS

Medium Weight Yarn **[4]**
[3 ounces, 158 yards
(85 grams, 144 meters) per skein]:
{4-5-5}{6-7-8} skeins
Straight knitting needles, size 8
(5 mm) **or** size needed for gauge
16" (40.5 cm) Circular knitting
needle, size 8 (5 mm)
Yarn needle
Sewing needle and matching
thread
⁵/₈" (16 mm) Buttons - 8

GAUGE: In pattern,
20 sts = 4¹/₂"(11.5 cm);
24 rows = 4" (10 cm)
blocked

Gauge Swatch: 4¹/₂"w x 4"h
(11.5 cm x 10 cm)
Cast on 20 sts.
Work same as Back for 24 rows.
Bind off all sts.

Techniques Used:
• YO **(Fig. 3, page 38)**
• K2 tog **(Fig. 6, page 39)**
• SSK **(Figs. 7a-c, page 39)**

BACK
BODY
With straight needles, cast on
{72-80-88}{100-108-116} sts.

Row 1 (Right side)**:** K5, P2, (K2, P2) across to last 5 sts, K5.

Row 2: K3, P2, (K2, P2) across to last 3 sts, K3.

Rows 3-6: Repeat Rows 1 and 2 twice.

Row 7: K3, P2, (K2, P2) across to last 3 sts, K3.

Row 8: K5, P2, (K2, P2) across to last 5 sts, K5.

Rows 9-12: Repeat Rows 7 and 8 twice.

Begin working in short rows for garter edge shaping.

Row 13: K3, **turn,** leave remaining sts unworked.

Row 14: K3, turn.

Row 15: K5, P2, (K2, P2) across to last 5 sts, K5.

Row 16: K3, turn, leave remaining sts unworked.

Row 17: K3, turn.

Row 18: K3, P2, (K2, P2) across to last 3 sts, K3.

Repeat Rows 3-18 for pattern until piece measures approximately {14-14-14}{16-16-16}"/ {35.5-35.5-35.5}{40.5-40.5-40.5} cm from cast on edge, ending by working Row 12.

ARMHOLE SHAPING
Maintain established pattern throughout.

Row 1: K9, P2, (K2, P2) across to last 9 sts, K9.

Row 2: K7, P2, (K2, P2) across to last 7 sts, K7.

Rows 3-6: Repeat Rows 1 and 2 twice.

Row 7: Bind off 4 sts, (K2, P2) across to last 7 sts, K7: {68-76-84} {96-104-112} sts.

Instructions continued on page 30.

fun & breezy

Row 8: Bind off 4 sts, K4, P2, (K2, P2) across to last 5 sts, K5: {64-72-80}{92-100-108} sts.

Repeat Rows 9-18 of Body once, then repeat Rows 3-18 for pattern until Armholes measure approximately {7-7^1/$_2$-8}{8^1/$_2$-9-9^1/$_2$}"/{18-19-20.5}{21.5-23-24} cm from bound off sts, ending by working a **wrong** side row.

Next Row: Bind off remaining sts on first side in pattern; with second yarn, work across.

Bind off remaining sts in pattern.

FRONT

Work same as Back until Front measures approximately {19-19^1/$_2$-20}{22^1/$_2$-23-23^1/$_2$}"/ {48.5-49.5-51}{57-58.5-59.5} cm from cast on edge, ending by working a **wrong** side row: {64-72-80}{92-100-108} sts.

NECK SHAPING

Both sides of Neck are worked at the same time, using separate yarn for each side. Maintain established pattern throughout.

Row 1: Work across first {22-26-29} {34-38-41} sts; with second yarn, bind off next {20-20-22} {24-24-26} sts, work across: {22-26-29}{34-38-41} sts **each** side.

Row 2: Work across; with second yarn, work across.

Row 3 (Decrease row)**:** Work across to within 3 sts of Neck edge, K2 tog, K1; with second yarn, K1, SSK, work across: {21-25-28}{33-37-40} sts **each** side.

Rows 4-11: Repeat Rows 2 and 3, 4 times: {17-21-24}{29-33-36} sts **each** side.

Work even until Armholes measure same as Back, ending by working a **wrong** side row.

Next Row: Bind off remaining sts on first side in pattern, leaving a long end for sewing; with second yarn, work across.

Bind off remaining sts in pattern, leaving a long end for sewing.

FINISHING

With long ends, sew shoulder seams.

NECKBAND

With **right** side facing and using circular needle, pick up {30-30-32} {34-34-36} sts evenly spaced across Back Neck edge *(Figs. 11a &b, page 40)*, pick up 12 sts across left Front Neck edge, pick up {20-20-22} {24-24-26} sts across bound off sts, pick up 12 sts across right Front Neck edge, place marker to mark beginning of round *(see Markers, page 38)*: {74-74-78}{82-82-86} sts.

Rnd 1: Purl around.

Rnd 2: Knit around.

Repeat Rnds 1 and 2 until Neckband measures 1" (2.5 cm), ending by working Rnd 1.

Bind off all sts in **knit**.

BUTTON TAB (Make 2)

With straight needles, cast on 11 sts.

Knit 6 rows.

Buttonhole Row: (K2, K2 tog, YO) twice, K3.

Knit every row until Tab measures 4" (10 cm) from cast on edge **or** to desired length.

Repeat Buttonhole Row.

Knit 5 rows.

Bind off all sts in **knit**.

Sew 2 buttons to Front at waist, 2" (5 cm) in from right and left side edges. Sew remaining 2 buttons approximately 1" (2.5 cm) above first 2 buttons.

Repeat for remaining 4 buttons on Back.

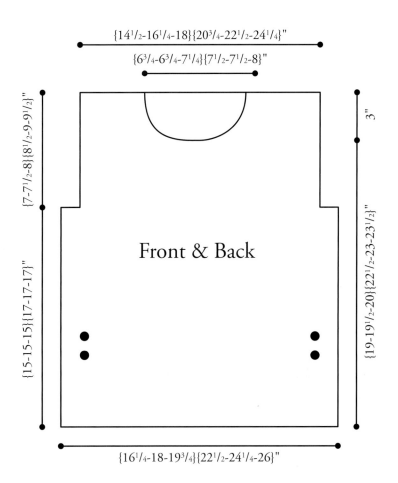

{14¹/₂-16¹/₄-18}{20³/₄-22¹/₂-24¹/₄}"

{6³/₄-6³/₄-7¹/₄}{7¹/₂-7¹/₂-8}"

{7-7¹/₂-8}{8¹/₂-9-9¹/₂}"

3"

{15-15-15}{17-17-17}"

Front & Back

{19-19¹/₂-20}{22¹/₂-23-23¹/₂}"

{16¹/₄-18-19³/₄}{22¹/₂-24¹/₄-26}"

something special

Size	Finished Chest Measurement
X-Small	31" (78.5 cm)
Small	35" (89 cm)
Medium	39" (99 cm)
Large	43" (109 cm)
X-Large	47" (119.5 cm)
2X-Large	51" (129.5 cm)

Size Note: Instructions are written with sizes X-Small, Small, and Medium in the first set of braces { } and sizes Large, X-Large, and 2X-Large in the second set of braces. Instructions will be easier to read if you circle all the numbers pertaining to your size. If only one number is given, it applies to all sizes.

MATERIALS

Medium Weight Yarn 🔵4
[3 ounces, 185 yards
(85 grams, 170 meters) per skein]:
   {4-4-5}{6-6-7} skeins
Straight knitting needles, size 8
   (5 mm) **or** size needed for gauge
Double pointed needles, size 8
   (5 mm) - for 3-needle bind off
   and I-cord
Cable needle
Stitch holders - 2
Marker
Yarn needle
Sewing needle and thread
Hook and eye set - 1

GAUGE: In Stockinette Stitch, (knit one row, purl one row) 20 sts and 24 rows = 4" (10 cm)

Techniques Used:
• K2 tog (*Fig. 6, page 39*)
• SSK (*Figs. 7a-c, page 39*)
• Adding new stitches (*Figs. 5a & b, page 39*)

STITCH GUIDE

FRONT CROSS (uses 4 sts)
Slip next 2 sts onto cable needle and hold in **front** of work, P2, K2 from cable needle.
BACK CROSS (uses 4 sts)
Slip next 2 sts onto cable needle and hold in **back** of work, K2, P2 from cable needle.

BACK

Cast on {80-90-100} {110-120-130} sts.

Beginning with a **knit** row, work in Stockinette Stitch until Back measures approximately {13³/₄-14¹/₂-15}{15-15-15¹/₄}"/ {35-37-38}{38-38-38.5} cm from cast on edge, ending by working a **purl** row.

ARMHOLE SHAPING

Maintain established pattern throughout.

Rows 1 and 2: Bind off {4-5-6} {7-9-10} sts, work across: {72-80-88} {96-102-110} sts.

Row 3 (Decrease row)**:** K1, SSK, knit across to last 3 sts, K2 tog, K1: {70-78-86}{94-100-108} sts.

Continue to decrease one stitch at **each** edge, every other row, {3-4-6} {7-8-10} times **more**: {64-70-74} {80-84-88} sts.

Work even until Armholes measure approximately {7-7¹/₄-7³/₄} {8¹/₄-8³/₄-9}"/{18-18.5-19.5} {21-22-23} cm, ending by working a **purl** row.

NECK SHAPING

Both sides of Neck are worked at the same time, using separate yarn for each side.

Row 1: Knit across first {18-21-21} {23-25-25} sts; with second yarn, bind off next {28-28-32}{34-34-38} sts, knit across: {18-21-21} {23-25-25} sts **each** side.

Rows 2-5: Work across; with second yarn, bind off 3 sts, work across: {12-15-15}{17-19-19} sts **each** side.

Instructions continued on page 34.

SHOULDER SHAPING

Rows 1 and 2: Bind off {6-7-7} {8-9-9} sts, work across; with second yarn, work across: {6-8-8} {9-10-10} sts **each** side.

Row 3: Bind off remaining sts on first side, leaving a long end for sewing; with second yarn, work across.

Bind off remaining sts, leaving a long end for sewing.

RIGHT FRONT

Cast on {47-52-57}{62-67-72} sts.

Row 1 (Right side)**:** K3, P4, K2, P2, K2, P4, place marker **(see Markers, page 38)**, knit across.

Row 2: Purl across to marker, K4, P2, K2, P2, K4, WYF slip last 3 sts as if to **purl.**

Knit the first 3 sts on each **right** side row with normal tension to obtain an edging similar to I-cord.

Row 3: K3, P2, work Back Cross, P2, work Front Cross, P2, knit across.

Row 4: Purl across to marker, K2, P2, K6, P2, K2, WYF slip last 3 sts as if to **purl.**

Row 5: K3, P2, K2, P6, K2, P2, knit across.

Rows 6-8: Repeat Rows 4 and 5 once, then repeat Row 4 once **more.**

Row 9: K3, P2, work Front Cross, P2, work Back Cross, P2, knit across.

Row 10: Purl across to marker, K4, P2, K2, P2, K4, WYF slip last 3 sts as if to **purl.**

Row 11: K3, P4, K2, P2, K2, P4, knit across.

Rows 12 and 13: Repeat Rows 10 and 11.

Repeat Rows 2-13 for pattern until Right Front measures same as Back to Armhole Shaping, ending by working a **right** side row.

ARMHOLE AND NECK SHAPING

Maintain established pattern throughout.

Row 1: Bind off {4-5-6} {7-9-10} sts, work across: {43-47-51} {55-58-62} sts.

Row 2 (Decrease row)**:** Work across to last 3 sts, K2 tog, K1: {42-46-50} {54-57-61} sts.

Row 3: Work across.

Rows 4-7: Repeat Rows 2 and 3 twice: {40-44-48}{52-55-59} sts.

Row 8 (Decrease row)**:** Work across to marker, SSK, work across to last 3 sts, K2 tog, K1: {38-42-46} {50-53-57} sts:

Continue to decrease one stitch at Armhole edge, every other row, {0-1-3}{4-5-7} time(s) **more (see Zeros, page 38)** AND AT THE SAME TIME decrease one stitch at Neck edge, every other row, {0-0-2} {3-1-4} time(s); then decrease every fourth row, {9-9-9}{9-11-10} times: {29-32-32}{34-36-36} sts.

Work even until Armhole measures approximately {8-8$^1/_4$-8$^3/_4$} {9$^1/_4$-9$^3/_4$-10}"/{20.5-21-22} {23.5-25-25.5} cm, ending by working a **right** side row.

SHOULDER SHAPING

Row 1: Bind off {6-7-7} {8-9-9} sts, work across: {23-25-25} {26-27-27} sts.

Row 2: Work across.

Row 3: Bind off {6-8-8}{9-10-10} sts, work across: 17 sts.

NECKBAND

Row 1 (Increase row)**:** Work across, **turn**; add on one st for edge st: 18 sts.

Work even keeping edge st in Stockinette Stitch until Neckband measures approximately {3-3-3$^1/_4$} {3$^1/_2$-3$^1/_2$-3$^3/_4$}/{7.5-7.5-8.5} {9-9-9.5} cm, ending by working a **wrong** side row.

Slip sts onto st holder.

LEFT FRONT

Cast on {47-52-57}{62-67-72} sts.

Row 1 (Right side)**:** Knit first {30-35-40}{45-50-55} sts, place marker, P4, K2, P2, K2, P4, K3.

Row 2: WYF slip first 3 sts as if to **purl,** K4, P2, K2, P2, K4, purl across.

Knit the last 3 sts on each **right** side row with normal tension to obtain an edging similar to I-cord.

Row 3: Knit across to marker, P2, work Back Cross, P2, work Front Cross, P2, K3.

Row 4: WYF slip first 3 sts as if to **purl**, K2, P2, K6, P2, K2, purl across.

Row 5: Knit across to marker, P2, K2, P6, K2, P2, K3.

Rows 6-8: Repeat Rows 4 and 5 once, then repeat Row 4 once **more**.

Row 9: Knit across to marker, P2, work Front Cross, P2, work Back Cross, P2, K3.

Row 10: WYF slip first 3 sts as if to **purl**, K4, P2, K2, P2, K4, purl across.

Row 11: Knit across to marker, P4, K2, P2, K2, P4, K3.

Rows 12 and 13: Repeat Rows 10 and 11.

Repeat Rows 2-13 for pattern until Left Front measures same as Right Front to Armhole Shaping, ending by working a **wrong** side row.

ARMHOLE AND NECK SHAPING

Maintain established pattern throughout.

Row 1: Bind off {4-5-6} {7-9-10} sts, work across: {43-47-51} {55-58-62} sts.

Row 2: Work across.

Row 3 (Decrease row): K1, SSK, work across: {42-46-50} {54-57-61} sts.

Row 4: Work across.

Rows 5 and 6: Repeat Rows 3 and 4: {41-45-49}{53-56-60} sts.

Row 7 (Decrease row): K1, SSK, work across to within 2 sts of marker, K2 tog, work across: {39-43-47} {51-54-58} sts.

Continue to decrease one stitch at Armhole edge, every other row, {1-2-4}{5-6-8} time(s) **more** AND AT THE SAME TIME decrease one stitch at Neck edge, every other row, {0-0-2}{3-1-4} time(s); then decrease every fourth row, {9-9-9}{9-11-10} times: {29-32-32}{34-36-36} sts.

Work even until Armhole measures same as Right Front to Shoulder Shaping, ending by working a **wrong** side row.

SHOULDER SHAPING AND NECKBAND

Work same as Right Front.

FINISHING

Sew shoulder seam.

Slip sts from st holders onto double pointed needles. With **right** sides together, join Neckbands together using the 3-needle bind off method **(Fig. 12, page 40)**.

Sew Neckband to Back Neck edge, easing as necessary to fit and making sure seam is centered.

Weave side seams **(Fig. 13, page 40)**.

Instructions continued on page 36.

TRIM
ARMHOLE

With double pointed needles, cast on 3 sts, ★ K2, slip 1 as if to **purl**, with **wrong** side facing, pick up one st along one Armhole edge *(Figs. 11a & b, page 40)*, pass slipped st over picked up st, slide sts to opposite end of needle; repeat from ★ around entire edge skipping rows or sts as necessary to keep the Trim from being too full.

Bind off all sts in **knit**; cut yarn leaving a long end for sewing.

With long end, sew ends of Trim together.

Repeat around second Armhole.

BOTTOM EDGE

With double pointed needles, cast on 3 sts, K2, slip 1 as if to **purl**, with **wrong** side facing, pick up one st at Right Front lower corner, pass slipped st over picked up st, slide sts to opposite end of needle, ★ K2, slip 1 as if to **purl**, pick up one st on bottom edge, pass slipped st over picked up st, slide sts to opposite end of needle; repeat from ★ across to Left Front lower corncr, skipping sts as necessary to keep the Trim from being too full.

Bind off all sts in **knit**.

Sew hook and eye to Fronts at beginning of Neck Shaping.

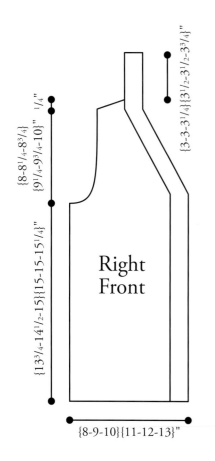

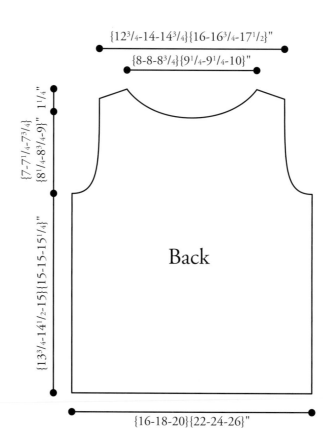

Note: Vest includes two edge stitches.

ABBREVIATIONS

cm	centimeters
K	knit
M1	make one
mm	millimeters
P	purl
PSSO	pass slipped stitch over
Rnd(s)	round(s)
SSK	slip, slip, knit
SSP	slip, slip, purl
st(s)	stitch(es)
tbl	through back loop(s)
tog	together
WYB	with yarn in back
WYF	with yarn in front
YO	yarn over

★ — work instructions following ★ as many **more** times as indicated in addition to the first time.

( ) or [ ] — work enclosed instructions **as many** times as specified by the number immediately following **or** contains explanatory remarks.

colon (:) — the number(s) given after a colon at the end of a row or round denote(s) the number of stitches you should have on that row or round.

work even — work without increasing or decreasing in the established pattern.

Yarn Weight Symbol & Names	LACE 0	SUPER FINE 1	FINE 2	LIGHT 3	MEDIUM 4	BULKY 5	SUPER BULKY 6
Type of Yarns in Category	Fingering, size 10 crochet thread	Sock, Fingering, Baby	Sport, Baby	DK, Light Worsted	Worsted, Afghan, Aran	Chunky, Craft, Rug	Bulky, Roving
Knit Gauge Range* in Stockinette St to 4" (10 cm)	33-40** sts	27-32 sts	23-26 sts	21-24 sts	16-20 sts	12-15 sts	6-11 sts
Advised Needle Size Range	000-1	1 to 3	3 to 5	5 to 7	7 to 9	9 to 11	11 and larger

KNIT TERMINOLOGY	
UNITED STATES	**INTERNATIONAL**
gauge =	tension
bind off =	cast off
yarn over (YO) =	yarn forward (yfwd) **or** yarn around needle (yrn)

*GUIDELINES ONLY: The chart above reflects the most commonly used gauges and needle sizes for specific yarn categories.

** Lace weight yarns are usually knitted on larger needles to create lacy openwork patterns. Accordingly, a gauge range is difficult to determine. Always follow the gauge stated in your pattern.

KNITTING NEEDLES																
U.S.	0	1	2	3	4	5	6	7	8	9	10	10½	11	13	15	17
U.K.	13	12	11	10	9	8	7	6	5	4	3	2	1	00	000	---
Metric - mm	2	2.25	2.75	3.25	3.5	3.75	4	4.5	5	5.5	6	6.5	8	9	10	12.75

■□□□ BEGINNER	Projects for first-time knitters using basic knit and purl stitches. Minimal shaping.
■■□□ EASY	Projects using basic stitches, repetitive stitch patterns, simple color changes, and simple shaping and finishing.
■■■□ INTERMEDIATE	Projects with a variety of stitches, such as basic cables and lace, simple intarsia, double-pointed needles and knitting in the round needle techniques, mid-level shaping and finishing.
■■■■ EXPERIENCED	Projects using advanced techniques and stitches, such as short rows, fair isle, more intricate intarsia, cables, lace patterns, and numerous color changes.

GAUGE

Exact gauge is **essential** for proper fit. Before beginning your project, make a sample swatch in the yarn and needle specified. After completing the swatch, measure it, counting your stitches and rows carefully. If your swatch is larger or smaller than specified, **make another, changing needle size to get the correct gauge.** Keep trying until you find the size needles that will give you the specified gauge. Once proper gauge is obtained, measure width of garment approximately every 3" (7.5 cm) to be sure gauge remains consistent. If you have more rows per inch than specified, use a larger size needle for the purl rows; if fewer, use a smaller size needle for the purl rows.

ZEROS

To consolidate the length of an involved pattern, zeros are sometimes used so that all sizes can be combined. For example, decrease every other row, 0{1-2} time(s) means the first size would do nothing, the second size would decrease once, and the largest size would decrease twice.

MARKERS

As a convenience to you, we have used markers to help distinguish the beginning of a pattern or a round. Place markers as instructed. You may use purchased markers or tie a length of contrasting color yarn around the needle. When you reach a marker on each row or round, slip it from the left needle to the right needle; remove it when no longer needed.

KNIT ONE THROUGH THE BACK LOOP
(abbreviated K1 tbl)

Insert the right needle into the **back** of next stitch from **front** to **back** (*Fig. 1*), then **knit** the stitch.

Fig. 1

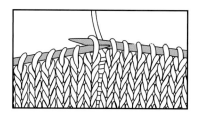

CHANGING COLORS

When changing colors, always pick up the new color yarn from beneath the dropped yarn and keep the color which has just been worked to the left (*Fig. 2*). This will prevent holes in the finished piece. Take extra care to keep your tension even.

Fig. 2

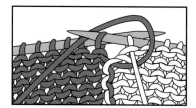

YARN OVER
(abbreviated YO)

Bring the yarn forward **between** the needles, then back **over** the top of the right hand needle, so that it is now in position to knit the next stitch (*Fig. 3*).

Fig. 3

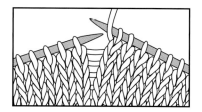

MAKE ONE
(abbreviated M1)

Insert the **left** needle under the horizontal strand between the stitches from the **front** (*Fig. 4a*). Then knit into the **back** of the strand (*Fig. 4b*).

Fig. 4a

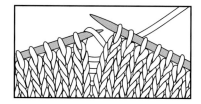

Fig. 4b

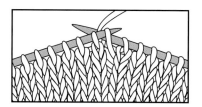

ADDING NEW STITCHES

Insert the right needle into stitch as if to **knit**, yarn over and pull loop through *(Fig. 5a)*, insert the left needle into the loop just worked from **front** to **back** and slip the loop onto the left needle *(Fig. 5b)*. Repeat for required number of stitches.

Fig. 5a

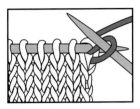

Fig. 5b

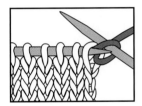

DECREASES
KNIT 2 TOGETHER
(abbreviated K2 tog)
Insert the right needle into the **front** of the first two stitches on the left needle as if to **knit** *(Fig. 6)*, then **knit** them together as if they were one stitch.

Fig. 6

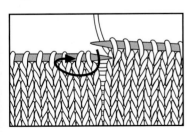

SLIP, SLIP, KNIT
(abbreviated SSK)
Slip the first stitch as if to **knit**, then slip the next stitch as if to **knit** *(Fig. 7a)*. Insert the left needle into the **front** of both slipped stitches *(Fig. 7b)* and **knit** them together as if they were one stitch *(Fig. 7c)*.

Fig. 7a

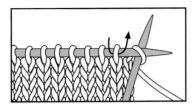

Fig. 7b

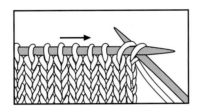

Fig. 7c

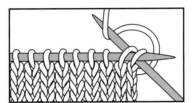

SLIP 1, KNIT 2 TOGETHER, PASS SLIPPED STITCH OVER
(abbreviated slip 1, K2 tog, PSSO)
Slip one stitch as if to **knit**. Knit the next two stitches together *(Fig. 6)*. With the left needle, bring the slipped stitch over the stitch just made *(Fig. 8)* and off the needle.

Fig. 8

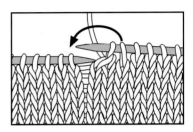

PURL 2 TOGETHER
(abbreviated P2 tog)
Insert the right needle into the **front** of the first two stitches on the left needle as if to **purl** *(Fig. 9)*, then **purl** them together as if they were one stitch.

Fig. 9

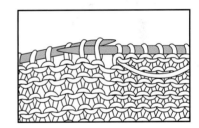

SLIP, SLIP, PURL
(abbreviated SSP)

Separately slip two stitches as if to **knit**. Place these two stitches **back** onto the left needle. Insert the right needle into the **back** of both stitches from **back** to **front** *(Fig. 10)* and **purl** them together as if they were one stitch.

Fig. 10

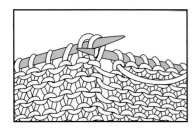

3-NEEDLE BIND OFF

Holding pieces with **right** sides together and needles parallel to each other, insert a third needle as if to **knit** into the first stitch on the front needle **and** into the first stitch on the back needle *(Fig. 12)*. **Knit** these two stitches together as if they were one stitch and slip them off the needle. ★ Knit the next stitch on each needle together and slip them off the needle. To bind off, insert the left needle into the first stitch on the right needle and pull the first stitch over the second stitch and off the right needle; repeat from ★ across until all of the stitches have been bound off.

Fig. 12

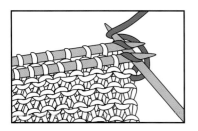

PICKING UP STITCHES

When instructed to pick up stitches, insert the needle from the **front** to the **back** under two strands at the edge of the worked piece *(Figs. 11a & b)*. Put the yarn around the needle as if to **knit**, then bring the needle with the yarn back through the stitch to the front, resulting in a stitch on the needle. Repeat this along the edge, picking up the required number of stitches. A crochet hook may be helpful to pull yarn through.

Fig. 11a

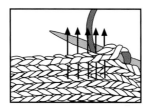

Fig. 11b

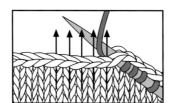

WEAVING SEAMS

With the **right** side of both pieces facing you and edges even, sew through both sides once to secure the seam. Insert the needle under the bar **between** the first and second stitches on the row and pull the yarn through *(Fig. 13)*. Insert the needle under the next bar on the second side and pull the yarn through. Repeat from side to side, being careful to match rows. If the edges are different lengths, it may be necessary to insert the needle under two bars at one edge.

Fig. 13

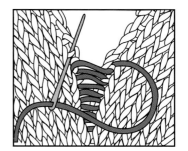